D1708940

DO YOU REALLY WANT TO MEET A SWAN?

WRITTEN BY CARI MEISTER   ILLUSTRATED BY DANIELE FABBRI

HICKMAN CO. LIBRARY SYSTEM
J.B. WALKER MEMORIAL LIBRARY
CENTERVILLE, TN 37033

Amicus Illustrated is published by Amicus
P.O. Box 1329, Mankato, MN 56002
www.amicuspublishing.us

Copyright © 2015 Amicus. International copyright
reserved in all countries. No part of this book
may be reproduced in any form without written
permission from the publisher.

Library of Congress Cataloging-in-Publication Data
Meister, Cari, author.
 Do you really want to meet a swan? / by Cari
Meister ; illustrated by Daniele Fabbri.
   pages cm. — (Do you really want to meet?)
 Summary: "A child goes on an adventure to a
marsh to observe a swan and discovers swans can
be dangerous if they're defending their nest"—
Provided by publisher.
 Audience: Grade K to 3.
 Includes bibliographical references and index.
 ISBN 978-1-60753-458-7 (library binding) —
ISBN 978-1-60753-673-4 (ebook)
 1. Swans—Juvenile literature. 2. Marshes—Juvenile
literature. I. Fabbri, Daniele, 1978- ill. II. Title.
 QL696.A52M45 2015
 598.4'18—dc23   2013034707

Editor: Rebecca Glaser
Designer: Kathleen Petelinsek

Printed in the United States of America at
Corporate Graphics in North Mankato, Minnesota.
10 9 8 7 6 5 4 3 2 1

ABOUT THE AUTHOR

Cari Meister is the author of more than 120 books for children, including the *Tiny* series and *My Pony Jack*. She lives in Evergreen, CO and Minnetrista, MN with her husband, John, their four sons, one dog, one horse, and 4 hamsters. You can visit her online at www.carimeister.com.

ABOUT THE ILLUSTRATOR

Daniele Fabbri was born in Ravenna, Italy, in 1978. He graduated from Istituto Europeo di Design in Milan, Italy, and started his career as a cartoon animator, storyboarder, and background designer for animated series. He has worked as a freelance illustrator since 2003, collaborating with international publishers and advertising agencies.

NAT BIRDS CENT

SWAN

S o I hear you want to meet a swan.
Swans certainly look beautiful and graceful . . .

. . . but did you know that swans have ENORMOUS wings that flap brutally at intruders? And that they hiss and peck viciously when protecting their young?

DO NOT GET TOO CLOSE
← TO
NESTING BIRDS

Do you STILL really want to meet a swan? All right. You will need a kayak and binoculars. Put a first aid kit in your kayak, just in case. Some people who get too close to swans end up with bruises or cuts.

Let's head to the marsh. This is
the perfect habitat for a swan.
TOOTOOT TOOTOOTOOT!

Did you hear that? That's the sound of the trumpeter swan. Trumpeter swans are one of largest swans. Males can weigh 30 pounds (14 kg).

Look! That swan is about to land.
Shh! We don't want to scare him
away. Paddle that way—toward
the shallower water.

Wait! What's that
white fluff over there?
Get the binoculars.

It's another swan! But what's she doing under the water? Is she eating? Swans eat tubers from underwater plants, but she's not eating that cattail. Watch out behind you!

WHAPP! WHAPPP!
WHAPP! HISSSS!!!!
Yikes! Quick! Paddle
the other way. That's
one ANGRY bird!
Don't mess with him.

Oh! He's defending his nest. Swans are very protective of their nests. While a female is laying eggs and when she sits on the nest, the male keeps guard. Males have been known to kill intruders, batting them to death with their wings.

Mute swans sometimes hold intruders
under the water and drown them.

Sound a little extreme? Well, swans live in an extreme world. Hungry bears and raccoons constantly try to steal their eggs.

Follow that swan with the cattail! But keep
a safe distance away. It's swimming toward
another swan. What are they doing?

They're building a nest—a huge nest! It's about 6 feet (1.8 m) across. They'll take their time to make it sturdy. Most swans mate for life. They will use the same nest year after year, if it is not flooded or destroyed.

Peep! Peep! Peep! A baby swan! Isn't he cute?
Baby swans are called cygnets. By the time they
are one year old, all of their fluffy gray feathers
will be gone. Now, you've really met a swan.

Just stay away from his dad!

WHERE DO SWANS LIVE?

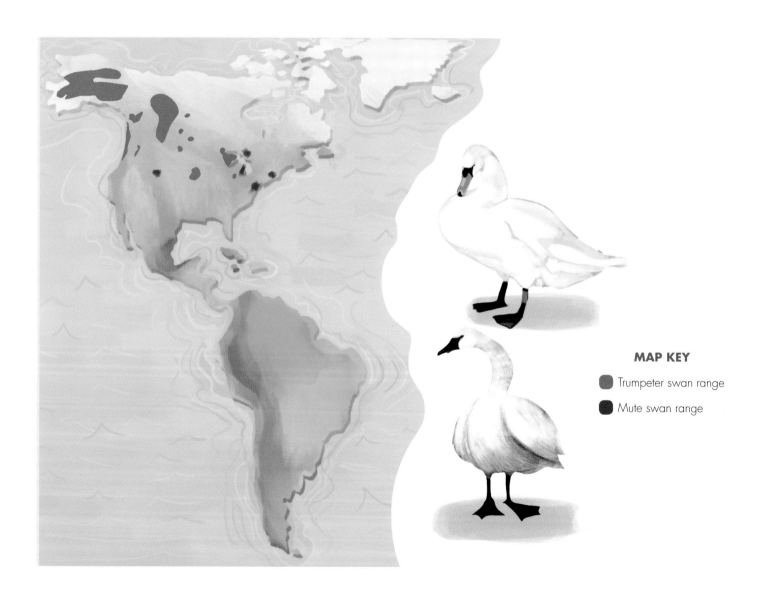

MAP KEY

⬤ Trumpeter swan range

⬤ Mute swan range

GLOSSARY

cygnet A baby swan.

habitat The place and natural conditions where an animal lives.

intruder An unwanted visitor.

marsh Land that is low, wet, and often treeless.

tuber A fleshy part of a plant stem that has small buds and leaves and usually grows underground or under water.

READ MORE

Bodden, Valerie. Swans. Amazing Animals. Mankato, Minn.: Creative Education, 2009.

Johnson, Jinny. River and Lake Life. Watery Worlds. Mankato, Minn.: Smart Apple Media, 2012.

Stewart, Melissa. Swans. New York: Marshall Cavendish Benchmark, 2008.

WEBSITES

BioKIDS—Kids' Inquiry of Diverse Species, Critter Catalog, Trumpeter Swan
https://animaldiversity.ummz.umich.edu/biokids/critters/Cygnus_buccinator/
View photos of trumpeter swans and read lots of facts about them. Great for reports.

EEK!—Critter Corner—The Trumpeter Swan
http://dnr.wi.gov/eek/critter/bird/trumpeterswan.htm
Learn to identify a trumpeter swan and its look-alikes.

Trumpeter Swan
http://www.birdweb.org/birdweb/bird/trumpeter_swan
Listen to the trumpeter swan's call and read facts about its habitat and behavior in the wild.

Every effort has been made to ensure that these websites are appropriate for children. However, because of the nature of the Internet, it is impossible to guarantee that these sites will remain active indefinitely or that their contents will not be altered.

HICKMAN CO. LIBRARY SYSTEM
J.B. WALKER MEMORIAL LIBRARY
CENTERVILLE, TN 37033